A Short-Term **DISCIPLE** Bible Study

INVITATION
TO
JOHN

LEADER GUIDE

D1219922

Abingdon Press
Nashville

A Short-Term DISCIPLE Bible Study

INVITATION TO JOHN
LEADER GUIDE

Copyright © 2007 by Abingdon Press

Harriett Jane Olson, Senior Vice President of Publishing and Editor of Church School Publications; Mark Price, Senior Editor; Mickey Frith, Associate Editor; Kent Sneed, Design Manager; Leonardo M. Ferguson, Designer

07 08 09 10 11 12 13 14 15 16 — 10 9 8 7 6 5 4 3 2 1

MANUFACTURED IN THE UNITED STATES OF AMERICA

Contents

Introducing
This Study Series

INVITATION TO JOHN is one of a series of studies developed on the model of DISCIPLE Bible study. DISCIPLE is a family of Bible study resources based on the general assumption that people are hungry for God's Word, for fellowship in prayer and study, and for biblically informed guidance in ministry. Like all long-term DISCIPLE resources, this series of short-term DISCIPLE Bible studies: (1) presents the Bible as the primary text; (2) calls for daily preparation on the part of students; (3) features a weekly meeting based on small-group discussion; (4) includes a video component for making available the insights of biblical scholars to set the Scriptures in context; and (5) has as one of its goals the enhancement of Christian discipleship.

INVITATION TO JOHN is designed to provide congregations with an in-depth, high-commitment Bible study resource able to be completed in a shorter time frame than the foundational DISCIPLE studies. However, the shorter time frame does not mean this study has expectations different from those associated with the thirty-four week DISCIPLE: BECOMING DISCIPLES THROUGH BIBLE STUDY. In fact, the term *invitation* rather than *introduction* has been used for this series to signal that these studies are not basic introductions but rather invitations to in-depth study. The expectation remains that participants will prepare for the weekly meeting by reading substantial portions of Scripture and taking notes. The expectation remains that group discussion, rather than lecture, will be the preferred learning approach. The expectation remains that biblical scholarship will be part of the group's study together. The expectation remains that each person's encounter with the Bible will call him or her to more faithful discipleship. In fact, it is our hope that this series of short-term DISCIPLE Bible studies will ultimately inspire participants to commit to a long-term DISCIPLE study in the future. For while these short studies of selected Scriptures can be both meaningful and convenient, the deeply transforming experience of reading and studying all the Scriptures—from Genesis to Revelation—continues to be the primary aim of DISCIPLE.

Leading This Study

For leaders of INVITATION TO JOHN, it will be vital to keep in mind that to have as rich and meaningful an experience as possible with this type of short-term study, you will need to pay close attention to the timing of the suggested discussion activities and group dynamics. One of the challenges of any short-term, small-group study—especially one based on group discussion—is the time it takes for people in the study to become comfortable sharing with one another. If your group is made up of people who are already acquainted, the challenge may be minimal. However, be prepared to have a group of people who do not know each other well, perhaps some who have never done much substantive Bible study and others who are graduates of long-term DISCIPLE studies. Different challenges—and rewards—will come as a result of the mix of people who make up your group(s). Make use of the following information as you prepare to lead INVITATION TO JOHN.

GROUP ORIENTATION

Plan to schedule an orientation meeting a week prior to the first weekly meeting. Take time then to make introductions, discuss the expectations of the study, distribute and review the materials, and preview the upcoming week's assignment. If necessary, consider discussing the kind of study Bible group members should use and taking time to make sure everyone is familiar with the aids in a study Bible. Have on hand several types of study Bibles for persons to look through.

WEEKLY SESSION

The times in parentheses beneath each section heading in the leader guide planning pages indicate the suggested number of minutes to allow for a particular activity. The first time is for use with a 60-minute meeting schedule, and the second time is for use with a 90-minute meeting schedule. Keep in mind that the discussion questions suggested for use in any one section may be more than enough to take up the allotted time. You will need to keep an eye on a clock and decide when and whether to move on. **The best way to gauge in advance how many questions to use and how long to allow discussion to last is to spend time answering the suggested questions yourself while preparing for the group session.** Be sure to do this, as well as preview the video—both Part 1 and 2—before the weekly session.

Gathering Around God's Word

(15–20 minutes)

Welcome

Begin on time by welcoming the group to the study. Ideally, this should be the *second* time the group has been together. During the orientation meeting the previous week, group participants met to preview the materials, discuss expectations of the study, and receive the assignment for the week. In case group participants who were not present at the orientation meeting arrive at this first session, be prepared to summarize as briefly as possible what they can expect from the study and what the study will expect from them.

Prayer

Establish a particular ritual of praying together at the start of the study. Keep in mind that the text of this study—the Bible—is a rich source of meaningful prayers. When appropriate, make use of other Bible translations when praying the Scriptures. Consider using some of Jesus' own prayers as recorded in John's Gospel: 11:41-42; 12:27; 17:11, 25-26.

Invitation From Scripture

At the close of the prayer time and just before introducing the first video segment, read aloud the focal verse of the session. The verse appears on the first page of each session in the participant book and is printed again in this section in the leader guide for each session. This reading is intended as an invitation to the session, serving to invoke God's presence and to give voice to the theme of the week's study.

Questions for Reflection

Follow up the reading aloud of the focal verse by presenting to the group the two questions in this section. You may want to read them aloud, or you may print them on a white board or on a sheet of paper for the group to see. Allow time for persons to consider the questions and then share briefly their responses in the total group.

Viewing the Video: Part 1

The video component in the series has two parts, and both are central to the group's study. In Part 1, a montage of images accompanies a dramatic reading of a passage from the week's assigned Scriptures. This video segment is designed to invite reflection and discussion of specific scenes in John's Gospel. The purpose of this video is to make available to the group a rich visual and aural experience of Scripture. The recommended procedure for using this video is as follows: (1) **Silence:** Group members should clear their minds in anticipation of receiving a new insight from a fresh hearing of God's Word. (2) **Listening:** Group members should pay attention to the images and listen carefully to the narrative—that is, experience the story unfold. (3) **Discussion:** Thoughtful discussion should follow careful listening. Use the set of questions that appear in this section for guiding the group's responses.

Encountering God's Word in the Text

(20–25 minutes)

In this section, group discussion centers around the assigned Scripture passages read and studied during the week. Note that the last set of questions listed for discussion is always the same and appears in boldface type:

❖ **In this week's readings, what did you "see" in Jesus? How did Jesus reveal God's glory? How do you understand Jesus as "the Word made flesh"?**

During discussion, be alert for ways to make use of the words or phrases that appear throughout the commentary as marginal notes within a gray background. That background is in the shape of the earliest known papyrus fragment of the Gospel of John. The fragment (P[52]) is part of the collection of Greek papyri held by the John Rylands University Library of Manchester, England.

Examining God's Word in Context

(15–20 minutes)

Viewing the Video: Part 2

The focus in this section is on viewing Part 2 of the video. This video features two conversations: The first one involves a biblical scholar (or scholars), and the second one takes place among a small group. Both conversations center around some portion of the week's readings in John and address a particular topic that emerges from them. One feature of each of the Part 2 video segments is an emphasis on a key "question" found in the text and an "invitation" or declaration that Jesus provides in response to that question. The idea is that the question asked in John expresses a question believers still ask today, in some way or another, seeking to understand who Jesus is and what kind of life he offers those who choose to follow him. Each pair of conversations is designed to prompt further discussion in your weekly study group. **Both conversations run back-to-back and are meant to be viewed without pausing between them.**

The experience of viewing this video segment is designed to place the week's readings in John in two contexts: (1) that of a scholar offering his or her insight into the texts and (2) that of a small group of people sharing their thoughts about the texts. On their own, the presentations may prompt sufficient discussion by the group. Simply following up the two conversations on the video with questions such as "What insight from scholar(s) or the small group caught your attention and why?" or "How did the conversation(s) inform your understanding of the week's reading?" may be enough to start and sustain a discussion. In addition, the instructions in this section provide other discussion options for use in following up the video segment.

Going Forth With God's Word: An Invitation to Discipleship

(10–15 minutes)

Consideration of the implications of the week's readings for Christian discipleship is the point of this section. The discussion questions in the leader guide for each session come from questions raised in the commentary and the "For Reflection" sections of the participant book. Be alert to additional questions that come to mind and might be useful at this time in the group meeting. As with any of these discussion questions, some will work better than others, and some will take more time to answer than others. Given the time frame for your weekly meeting, you may not have time to work through all the questions in the leader guide. Choose those you think will work best for your group, or make up your own.

Closing and Prayer

Turn to the next session and preview the lesson and assignments for the week ahead. Establish a pattern of inviting prayer concerns and praying together at this time.

GROUP DYNAMICS

The effectiveness of the group's study together depends heavily upon the way you as the leader manage individual participation. Plan for the majority of the weekly discussion to take place in smaller groups of two to four. Smaller groupings will give everyone more opportunity to talk and are the best way for people to get to know one another quickly. They also reduce the possibility that a couple of people will dominate the conversation or that some will not contribute at all. Smaller groupings communicate that preparation is expected and essential for fruitful discussion.

Also key to the effectiveness of the group's study together is how you manage your role as the leader. Remember that your primary role is to facilitate the process, not to provide the information. To that end, follow these basic guidelines as you lead the study:

- Prepare exactly as participants would prepare; see yourself as a learner among learners.

- Know where the discussion is heading from the outset; this will minimize the chances of getting sidetracked along the way.

- Set ground rules for group participation and maintenance early on; doing so will encourage the whole group to take responsibility for monitoring itself.

- Be a good listener; don't be afraid of silence. Allow time for people to think before responding.

Additional Resources

Your group will need only the Bible and the participant book to have a meaningful experience with this study. However, if your group should encounter unfamiliar terms and concepts or would like more information about some biblical text or topic, be prepared to suggest or to bring in additional reference materials for them to use. You may choose to include additional research or study activities in your plan for the weekly meeting, or you may assign group members to make use of these other reference materials outside of the meeting time and to report briefly to the group.

Several resources—including versions in print, CD-ROM, and video—are recommended as follows:

Bibles

One of the ways to enhance people's reading and understanding of the Bible is to have them read from more than one translation. Plan to have several study Bible versions available in the meeting room. In addition, encourage your group to read the Bible with curiosity, to ask *Who? What? Where? When? How?* and *Why?* as they read. Remind your group to let the Scripture speak for itself, even if the apparent meaning is troubling or unclear. Affirm both asking questions of Scripture as well as seeking answers to those questions in Scripture itself.

Bible Dictionaries

- *Eerdmans Dictionary of the Bible*, edited by David Noel Freedman (Wm. B. Eerdmans Publishing Company, 2000).

- *The HarperCollins Bible Dictionary*, edited by Paul J. Achtemeier (HarperSanFrancisco, 1996).

- *Dictionary of Jesus and the Gospels*, edited by Joel B. Green and Scot McKnight (InterVarsity Press, 1992).

Introductory Resources

- *Introducing the New Testament: Its Literature and Theology*, by Paul J. Achtemeier, Joel B. Green, and Marianne Meye Thompson (Wm. B. Eerdmans Publishing Company, 2001).

Biblical Commentaries

- *The New Interpreter's Bible: A Commentary in Twelve Volumes*, Vol. IX, the commentary on John (Abingdon Press, 1995). Also available in a CD-ROM edition.

- *John*, in Interpretation: A Bible Commentary for Teaching and Preaching, by Gerard S. Sloyan (John Knox Press, 1988).

- *John: The Maverick Gospel*, revised edition, by Robert Kysar (Westminster John Knox Press, 1993).

Film

- *The Gospel of John*, The Visual Bible series, 2003 (website: http://www.visualbible.com).

Art and Archaeology Related to the Bible

- *Archaeological Study Bible*, New International Version (The Zondervan Corporation, 2005).

- *The Biblical World in Pictures*, revised edition, CD-ROM (Biblical Archaeological Society).

- *The Life and World of Jesus the Messiah: Overview of the Gospels*, DVD (Preserving Bible Times, Inc., 2003). For more information, go to http://www.preservingbibletimes.org/content1.asp and click on "DVD Products."

Come and See

Gathering Around God's Word

(15–20 minutes)

Welcome

Begin on time by welcoming the group to the study. Ideally this should be the second time the group has been together. During the orientation meeting the previous week, group participants met to preview the material, discuss expectations of the study, and receive the assignment for the week. In case group participants who were not present at the orientation meeting arrive at the first session, be prepared to summarize as briefly as possible what they can expect from the study and what the study will expect from them.

Prayer

Establish a particular ritual of praying together at the start of the study. Keep in mind that the text of this study—the Bible—is a rich source of meaningful prayers. When appropriate, make use of other Bible translations when praying the Scriptures. Consider using some of Jesus' own prayers as recorded in John's Gospel: 11:41-42; 12:27; 17:11, 25-26.

Invitation From Scripture

When Jesus turned and saw them following, he said to them, "What are you looking for?" They said to him, "Rabbi" (which translated means Teacher), "where are you staying?" He said to them, "Come and see." —John 1:38-39

Questions for Reflection

- How would you describe the image of Jesus you see in this week's readings from John?

- How would you answer Jesus' question "What are you looking for?"

Viewing the Video: Session 1, Part 1

The video component in the series has two parts, and both are central to the group's study. In Part 1, a montage of images accompanies a dramatic reading of a passage from the week's assigned Scriptures. This video segment is designed to invite reflection and discussion of specific scenes in John's Gospel. The purpose of this video is to make available to the group a rich, visual, and aural experience of Scripture. The recommended procedure for using this video is as follows: (1) **Silence:** Group members should clear their minds in anticipation of receiving a new insight from a fresh hearing of God's Word. (2) **Listening:** Group members should pay attention to the images and listen carefully to the narrative—that is, experience the story unfold. (3) **Discussion:** Thoughtful discussion should follow careful listening. Use the following set of questions for guiding the group's responses.

John 1:35-51

• What feelings did the images evoke for you?

• How did the art you viewed "interpret" the Scripture you heard?

• What new insight(s) into the passage did the video provide?

Encountering God's Word in the Text

(20–25 minutes)

The readings this week introduce us to the Jesus in John's Gospel and to the kind of life Jesus offers those who choose to follow him. Call attention to the instructions under the Day 2 assignment on page 14 of the participant book. As a total group, talk about the differences among all four Gospel writers' introductions of Jesus. Then listen to what persons wrote down as their summary of John 1:1-18.

Next, in groups of three or four, discuss the following questions:

• How does the Prologue in John prepare the reader for how John will tell the rest of the Jesus story?

• In reading the accounts of John the Baptizer in each of the Gospels, what does each writer seem to claim as essential features of the Baptizer?

- What unique contribution to our understanding of Jesus does John the Baptizer make?

- Why do you think there is no mention in John of Jesus' baptism?

Listen to John 2:1-11 read aloud in the total group. Then ask:

- In this story, what elements appeal to the senses of smell, taste, touch, sound, and sight? What insights, if any, into the meaning of the narrative does attention to sensory details provide?

- If a sign is "a deed by means of which Jesus shows his true identity" (see page 21 in the participant book), then what do the actions of Jesus in John 1 and 2—calling followers, changing water into wine at a wedding, driving out money changers from the Temple—reveal about Jesus' identity?

❖ **In this week's readings, what did you "see" in Jesus? How did Jesus reveal God's glory? How do you understand Jesus as "the Word made flesh"?**

Examining God's Word in Context

(15–20 minutes)

In the Gospel of John, Jesus' words "come and see" suggest something more than a place on a map. The destination of a journey with Jesus cannot be understood ahead of time but can only be experienced along the way.

Viewing the Video: Session 1, Part 2

The focus in this section is on viewing Part 2 of the video. This video features two conversations: The first one involves biblical scholar Jaime Clark-Soles, and the second one takes place among a small group. Both conversations center around some portion of the week's readings in John and address a particular topic that emerges from them. One feature of each of the Part 2 video segments is an emphasis on a key "question" in the text and an "invitation" or declaration that Jesus provides in response to that question. The idea is that the question asked in John expresses a question believers still ask today, in some way or another, seeking to understand who Jesus is and what kind of life he offers those who choose to follow him. Each pair of conversations is designed to prompt further discussion in your weekly study group. **Both conversations run back-to-back and are meant to be viewed without pausing between them.**

Prepare to View Video

Note the context of the question directed toward Jesus in John 1:38, "Where are you staying?" and Jesus' invitation in John 1:39, "Come and see." Have group members locate the two verses in their Bibles before starting the video.

Discuss After Viewing Video

The experience of viewing this video segment is designed to place the week's readings in John in two contexts: (1) that of a scholar offering his or her insight into the texts and (2) that of a small group of people sharing their thoughts about the texts. On their own, the presentations may prompt sufficient discussion by the group. Simply following up the two conversations on the video with questions such as "What insight from scholar(s) or the small group caught your attention and why?" or "How did the conversation(s) inform your understanding of the week's reading?" may be enough to start and sustain a discussion. In addition, consider using the following questions for further discussion:

- Imagine yourself being addressed by Jesus with the question "What are you seeking?" What would your response be?

- In what way is Jesus' invitation to "come and see" an invitation to trust and a call to action? What kind of trust? What kind of action?

- When Jesus asked the two disciples, "What are you looking for?" they responded by asking, "Where are you staying?" What do you think they were expecting in response to their question?

Going Forth With God's Word: An Invitation to Discipleship

(10–15 minutes)

Like the first disciples, we are invited to "come and see"—to venture on a journey with Jesus and our Christian community. In pairs, discuss the following questions:

- What did you discover when you responded to Jesus' invitation to "come and see"?

• What signs have you seen in your life? How would you describe your own call to discipleship?

Call attention to the "For Reflection" section on page 23 in the participant book. Ask pairs to share responses to the questions.

If time permits, conclude this section of the group meeting by inviting persons to share their thoughts about the information printed in the participant book on page 24 under "For Further Reflection."

Closing and Prayer

Turn to Session 2, and review the focus of the lesson and the assignments for the week ahead. Establish a pattern of inviting prayer concerns and praying together at this time.

How Is It Possible?

(15–20 minutes)

Welcome
Begin on time by welcoming the group to the study.

Prayer
Pray together as you begin your study.

Invitation From Scripture
Jesus answered, "Very truly, I tell you, no one can enter the kingdom of God without being born of water and Spirit." … Nicodemus said to him, "How can these things be?" —John 3:5, 9

Questions for Reflection
- How would you describe the image of Jesus you see in this week's readings from John?

- What do Jesus' words to Nicodemus in 3:5 mean to you?

Viewing the Video: Session 2, Part 1
Follow this procedure for using this video: **Silence:** Clear your mind in anticipation of receiving a new insight from a fresh hearing of God's Word. **Listening:** Pay attention to the images and listen carefully to the narrative. **Discussion:** Use the following set of questions for guiding the group's responses.

John 4:1-30
- What feelings did the images evoke for you?

- How did the art you viewed "interpret" the Scripture you heard?

- What new insight(s) into the passage did the video provide?

Encountering God's Word in the Text

(20–25 minutes)

Condemnation is not so much a miserable eternity in a hell as it is a pointless life without true purpose and direction. In groups of three or four, look at the encounter Jesus had with Nicodemus in John 3:1-21. Examine the following themes and how they play out in the course of the narrative. Then discuss what each thematic pair contributes to our understanding of Jesus' message in John.

Darkness and light

Seeing and not seeing

Birth and rebirth

Knowledge and understanding

Earthly things and heavenly things

Death and eternal life

- How would you characterize Nicodemus?

- The Gospel of John does not include the story of Jesus' baptism. What does the absence of the baptism episode say about John's image of Jesus? About Jesus' purpose?

- How does John the Baptizer's response in John 3:27-36 relate to the issue of purification? How does it compare to the themes of sowing and reaping in John 4:31-38?

❖ **In this week's readings, what did you "see" in Jesus? How did Jesus reveal God's glory? How do you understand Jesus as "the Word made flesh"?**

Examining God's Word in Context

(15–20 minutes)

The Samaritan woman's proclamation about Jesus does not initially lead her fellow villagers to faith but rather leads them to encounter Jesus for themselves.

Viewing the Video: Session 1, Part 2

The focus in this section is on viewing Part 2 of the video. This video features two conversations: The first one involves biblical scholar Susan Hylen, and the second one takes place among a small group. Both conversations center around some portion of the week's readings in John and address a particular topic that emerges from them. One feature of each of the Part 2 video segments is an emphasis on a key "question" in the text and an "invitation" or declaration that Jesus provides in response to that question. **Both conversations run back-to-back and are meant to be viewed without pausing between them.**

Prepare to View Video

Note the context of the question directed toward Jesus in John 4:11, "Where do you get that living water?" and Jesus' response in 4:14, "The water that I will give will become in them a spring of water gushing up to eternal life." Have group members locate the two verses in their Bibles before starting the video. Listen for what is said about the contrast between Jesus' encounter with the Samaritan woman and with Nicodemus.

Discuss After Viewing Video

Follow up the two conversations in the video with questions such as "What insight from the scholar(s) or the small group caught your attention and why?" or "How did the conversation(s) inform your understanding of the week's reading?" In addition, consider using the following questions for further discussion.

Compare the encounters of Nicodemus and the Samaritan woman with Jesus.

- What characterizes them?

- How do the encounters address the question "Where do you get that living water?"

- How do the encounters address the question "How is it possible?"

The image of living water helped those listening to connect with Jesus' invitation to receive this living water.

- In what ways do we become conduits of Jesus' living water?

- In what ways do we hold back its flow?

- What other images would communicate this same message to believers today?

Going Forth With God's Word: An Invitation to Discipleship

(10–15 minutes)

Both John the Baptizer and the Samaritan woman stand out as living responses to Nicodemus' troubled inquiry "How is it possible?" In pairs, discuss the following questions:

- What are key events in your life that point beyond yourself and testify to God's presence and love?

- What sustains you in your own walk of faith? Of the characters in the readings this week, which one characterizes where you are in your walk of faith?

- How do you experience what Jesus means by the "living water"? How do you share it with others?

- When have you asked, "How is it possible?"

Call attention to the "For Reflection" section on page 34 in the participant book. Ask pairs to share responses to the questions.

If time permits, conclude this section of the group meeting by inviting persons to share their thoughts about the information printed in the participant book on page 35 under "For Further Reflection."

Closing and Prayer

Turn to Session 3, and review the focus of the lesson and the assignments for the week ahead. Establish a pattern of inviting prayer concerns and praying together at this time.

Taste for Yourself

Gathering Around God's Word

(15–20 minutes)

Welcome
Begin on time by welcoming the group to the study.

Prayer
Pray together as you begin your study.

Invitation From Scripture
[Jesus said,] "The bread of God is that which comes down from heaven and gives life to the world." They said to him, "Sir, give us this bread always."
—John 6:33-34

Questions for Reflection
- How would you describe the image of Jesus you see in this week's readings from John?

- In a country where materialism has a strong hold, bread is seldom seen as one of the basics of life. In light of this, how can the idea of Jesus being the bread of life have meaning in our culture and in your life?

Viewing the Video: Session 3, Part 1
Follow this procedure for using this video: **Silence:** Clear your mind in anticipation of receiving a new insight from a fresh hearing of God's Word. **Listening:** Pay attention to the images and listen carefully to the narrative. **Discussion:** Use the following set of questions for guiding the group's responses.

John 6:1-14, 25-40
- What feelings did the images evoke for you?

- How did the art you viewed "interpret" the Scripture you heard?

- What new insight(s) into the passage did the video provide?

Encountering God's Word in the Text

(20–25 minutes)

The readings this week make outrageous claims for Jesus and who he is. In a sense, they invite us to taste for ourselves and internalize Christ and his message.

Listen to John 5:1-15 read aloud in the total group. Then form groups of three or four to examine the story and discuss the following questions:

- Why does Jesus ask the question "Do you want to be made well?"

- How do you understand the lame man's response?

- Following his healing, how do the Jews respond? Why does Jesus look for the healed man? What is your understanding of Jesus' statement to him when he says, "Do not sin any more, so that nothing worse happens to you"?

Listen to John 5:16-47 read aloud in the total group. Then, in new groups of three or four, discuss the following questions:

- How does this story help us in our understanding of Jesus' authority?

- How does Jesus defend his authority?

- In your own life, what is your understanding of Jesus' authority, and to what witness do you appeal to defend his authority?

❖ **In this week's readings, what did you "see" in Jesus? How did Jesus reveal God's glory? How do you understand Jesus as "the Word made flesh"?**

Examining God's Word in Context

(15–20 minutes)

In the Gospel of John, bread is a metaphor of the nourishment, sustenance, and energy that changes one's whole life.

Viewing the Video: Session 3, Part 2

The focus in this section is on viewing Part 2 of the video. This video features two conversations: The first one involves biblical scholar Ben

Witherington, and the second one takes place among a small group. Both conversations center around some portion of the week's readings in John and address a particular topic that emerges from them. One feature of each of the Part 2 video segments is an emphasis on a key "question" in the text and an "invitation" or declaration that Jesus provides in response to that question. **Both conversations run back-to-back and are meant to be viewed without pausing between them.**

Prepare to View Video

Note the context of the question directed toward Jesus in John 6:30, "What sign are you going to give us then?" and Jesus' response in John 6:35, "I am the bread of life." Have group members locate the two verses in their Bibles before starting the video. Listen for what is said about the theme of "signs" in John and how people respond to what they see as Jesus' signs.

Discuss After Viewing Video

Follow up the two conversations in the video with questions such as "What insight from the scholar(s) or the small group caught your attention and why?" or "How did the conversation(s) inform your understanding of the week's reading?" In addition, consider using the following questions for further discussion.

- What does it mean that John's Gospel presents Jesus as "wisdom come in the flesh"?

Jesus' invitation to taste of "the bread of life" is an invitation to experience Christ in all his fullness. The world desires a sign, yet Christ offers abundant life.

- What form does our demand for a sign or proof take today?

- When have we been guilty of asking Jesus, "What have you done for me lately?"

Going Forth With God's Word: An Invitation to Discipleship

(10–15 minutes)

Discipleship is not a "lone-ranger" witness; rather, it is participating in a wide community of other witnesses, both present and past. In pairs, discuss the following questions:

- Why do you think individuals are not satisfied with Christ and long for another "sign"?

- What are ways you have tasted Christ and experienced him as "the bread of life"?

Call attention to the "For Reflection" section on page 46 in the participant book. Ask pairs to share responses to the questions.

If time permits, conclude this section of the group meeting by inviting persons to share their thoughts about the information printed in the participant book on page 47 under "For Further Reflection."

Closing and Prayer

Turn to Session 4, and review the focus of the lesson and the assignments for the week ahead. Establish a pattern of inviting prayer concerns and praying together at this time.

To Believe or Not to Believe

Gathering Around God's Word

(15–20 minutes)

Welcome

Begin on time by welcoming the group to the study.

Prayer

Pray together as you begin your study.

Invitation From Scripture

There was considerable complaining about him among the crowds. While some were saying, "He is a good man," others were saying, "No, he is deceiving the crowd." —John 7:12

Questions for Reflection

- How would you describe the image of Jesus you see in this week's readings from John?

- In what circumstances or among what crowds today do you still hear "considerable complaining" about Jesus?

Viewing the Video: Session 4, Part 1

Follow this procedure for using this video: **Silence:** Clear your mind in anticipation of receiving a new insight from a fresh hearing of God's Word. **Listening:** Pay attention to the images and listen carefully to the narrative. **Discussion:** Use the following set of questions for guiding the group's responses.

John 8:13a, 19-20, 31-47, 52-59

- What feelings did the images evoke for you?

- How did the art you viewed "interpret" the Scripture you heard?

- What new insight(s) into the passage did the video provide?

Encountering God's Word in the Text

(20–25 minutes)

The readings this week make clear the division between those who believed Jesus to be the Messiah and those who did not. The conversations in both John 7 and 8 share a Temple setting and allow us to listen to Jesus proclaim his understanding of who he is and how he came to be.

In groups of three or four, discuss the following questions related to John 7:

• Note the actions and attitudes of the individuals and groups in the text (Jesus' brothers, the Jews, the people of Jerusalem, the chief priests and Pharisees, the Temple police, Nicodemus, and Jesus). How does each character or group of characters highlight an aspect of Jesus' identity, and what role do they each play in the story?

• In light of your discussion, what is meant when Christ says, "My time has not yet come"?

Then, in those same groups, discuss these questions related to John 8:

• Jesus affirms his authority by appealing to the analogy of witnesses giving testimony in a legal proceeding. How is Jesus' use of that analogy important, especially in John's account?

• Along with Pharisees and other Jews, Jesus addresses "Jews who had believed in him." What is it that these Jews cannot accept about Jesus?

• To what extent do you think Jesus' opponents misunderstand rather than reject Jesus' claims about himself?

Finally, in the total group, read aloud John 8:1-11 and discuss these questions:

• What does this story say about Jesus' identity? What does the story say about forgiveness and reconciliation?

• What does Jesus' admonition "Go your way, and from now on do not sin again" say about the Gospels' view of second chances and judgment?

• How does our response to one who has sinned against us affect our own identity?

❖ In this week's readings, what did you "see" in Jesus? How did Jesus reveal God's glory? How do you understand Jesus as "the Word made flesh"?

Examining God's Word in Context

(15–20 minutes)

According to John's Gospel, if we want to find God, the answer is to seek out the incarnation of the divine Word, Jesus of Nazareth.

Viewing the Video: Session 4, Part 2

The focus in this section is on viewing Part 2 of the video. This video features two conversations: The first one involves biblical scholar Susan Hylen, and the second one takes place among a small group. Both conversations center around some portion of the week's readings in John and address a particular topic that emerges from them. One feature of each of the Part 2 video segments is an emphasis on a key "question" in the text and an "invitation" or declaration that Jesus provides in response to that question. **Both conversations run back-to-back and are meant to be viewed without pausing between them.**

Prepare to View Video

Note the context of the question directed toward Jesus in John 8:19, "Where is your Father?" and Jesus' response in John 8:58, "Before Abraham was, I am." Have group members locate the two verses in their Bibles before starting the video. Listen for what is said about why people could not accept Jesus' identity.

Discuss After Viewing Video

Follow up the two conversations in the video with questions such as "What insight from the scholar(s) or the small group caught your attention and why?" or "How did the conversation(s) inform your understanding of the week's reading?" In addition, consider using the following questions for further discussion.

- What exactly does John accomplish by setting episodes in Jesus' story during certain Jewish festivals?

- Why is it important for John to connect the promises of God to Israel with the promises of God in Jesus?

- Why do the religious leaders have such a hard time with Jesus' claims about himself? Why do we?

- What does Jesus' frequent use of the statement *I am* contribute to John's portrayal of both Jesus and Jesus' opponents?

- In what ways does Jesus' invitation to see him as God in the flesh still involve risk for us as believers today?

Going Forth With God's Word: An Invitation to Discipleship

(10–15 minutes)

Our discipleship necessitates that we ask daily, "Whose are we?" In pairs, discuss the following questions:

- Who is the source of being from whom we derive our identity?

- How can family ancestry or religious tradition get in the way of our relationship with God?

- What opposition have you encountered simply because you identify yourself as a Christian?

Call attention to the "For Reflection" section on page 58 in the participant book. Ask pairs to share responses to the questions.

If time permits, conclude this section of the group meeting by inviting persons to share their thoughts about the information printed in the participant book on page 59 under "For Further Reflection."

Closing and Prayer

Turn to Session 5, and review the focus of the lesson and the assignments for the week ahead. Establish a pattern of inviting prayer concerns and praying together at this time.

Are We Blind?

Gathering Around God's Word

(15–20 minutes)

Welcome
Begin on time by welcoming the group to the study.

Prayer
Pray together as you begin your study.

Invitation From Scripture
When he [Jesus] had said this, he spat on the ground and made mud with the saliva and spread the mud on the [blind] man's eyes.... Then he went and washed and came back able to see. —John 9:6-7

Questions for Reflection
- How would you describe the image of Jesus you see in this week's readings from John?

- From a spiritual point of view, how would you explain the difference between darkness and light?

Viewing the Video: Session 5, Part 1
Follow this procedure for using this video: **Silence:** Clear your mind in anticipation of receiving a new insight from a fresh hearing of God's Word. **Listening:** Pay attention to the images and listen carefully to the narrative. **Discussion:** Use the following set of questions for guiding the group's responses.

John 9:1-41
- What feelings did the images evoke for you?

- How did the art you viewed "interpret" the Scripture you heard?

- What new insight(s) into the passage did the video provide?

Encountering God's Word in the Text

(20–25 minutes)

In our complicated world, the search for the "middle way" seems the only way. However, when it comes to the kind of God we follow, there are only two ways to go and no path in between. Either commit to God's love in Christ or join forces to repress that love.

One of the intriguing aspects of the story of the man born blind is that when Jesus meets the man after his healing, Jesus uses the expression *Son of Man* in speaking of himself. Review the Day 3 assignment and the list of other instances in John's Gospel where the term *Son of Man* appears: 1:51; 3:13, 14; 5:27; 6:27, 53, 62; 8:28; 12:23; 13:31.

- What is this term meant to convey about Jesus in John's Gospel?

- How do you think this claim to be the "Son of Man" by Jesus in 9:35 is related to what he says in John 9:39?

- In Jesus' healing of the man born blind, what is the good news for the world?

In the total group, listen to John 10:1-18 read aloud. During the reading, note mental images that come to mind. Form groups of three or four and have them share with one another what images come to mind. Talk specifically about the positive and negative connotations of Christ as the "good shepherd" and his followers as sheep.

- How did the Scripture in John compare with images of sheep and shepherds in the other Scriptures recommended in the week's readings?

- Thinking of Jesus' mission and purpose as expressed in John 10:19-42, what does it mean that John has set the message in the context of the Festival of the Dedication (Hanukkah)?

❖ **In this week's readings, what did you "see" in Jesus? How did Jesus reveal God's glory? How do you understand Jesus as "the Word made flesh"?**

Examining God's Word in Context

(15–20 minutes)

The blind man provides us with a portrait of someone whose encounter with Jesus emboldens him to challenge the powers of his own religious establishment.

Viewing the Video: Session 5, Part 2

The focus in this section is on viewing Part 2 of the video. This video features two conversations: The first one involves biblical scholar Craig Koester, and the second one takes place among a small group. Both conversations center around some portion of the week's readings in John and address a particular topic that emerges from them. One feature of each of the Part 2 video segments is an emphasis on a key "question" in the text and an "invitation" or declaration that Jesus provides in response to that question. **Both conversations run back-to-back and are meant to be viewed without pausing between them.**

Prepare to View Video

Note the context of the question directed toward Jesus in John 9:2, "Who sinned...that he was born blind?" and Jesus' response in John 9:5, "I am the light of the world." Have group members locate the two verses in their Bibles before starting the video. Listen for what is said about the images of darkness and light and seeing and blindness in the story of the man born blind.

Discuss After Viewing Video

Follow up the two conversations in the video with questions such as "What insight from the scholar(s) or the small group caught your attention and why?" or "How did the conversation(s) inform your understanding of the week's reading?" In addition, consider using the following questions for further discussion.

- What is your understanding of God's role in human illness and divine healing?

- How do you understand the relationship between illness and sin?

- What connection is John trying to establish among the ideas of blindness, darkness, and unbelief?

- What do you make of the fact that the blind man, once healed, does not actually see Jesus until the end of the story?

- Which characters in the story do you relate to and why?

When Jesus says, "I am the light of the world," he offers us an alternative view of living in the world.

- How does his promise challenge and encourage us when we find ourselves blinded by the promises of our own success or selfishness?

- How can the church appear blind to the world? When this occurs, what should be our response as church members?

Going Forth With God's Word: An Invitation to Discipleship

(10–15 minutes)

How we follow Jesus invariably has its roots in how we understand Jesus. In pairs, discuss the following questions:

- What convinced you that Jesus is the Son of God? (His testimony in the Scriptures? His works in the lives of others? His works in your own life?)

- Share a moment in your life when you felt you were in spiritual darkness.

- How has Jesus been the light of your world?

Call attention to the "For Reflection" section on page 71 in the participant book. Ask pairs to share responses to the questions.

If time permits, conclude this section of the group meeting by inviting persons to share their thoughts about the information printed in the participant book on page 72 under "For Further Reflection."

Closing and Prayer

Turn to Session 6, and review the focus of the lesson and the assignments for the week ahead. Establish a pattern of inviting prayer concerns and praying together at this time.

I Couldn't Believe My Eyes!

Gathering Around God's Word

(15–20 minutes)

Welcome
Begin on time by welcoming the group to the study.

Prayer
Pray together as you begin your study.

Invitation From Scripture
Many...who had come with Mary and had seen what Jesus did, believed in him. But some of them went to the Pharisees and told them what he had done.
—John 11:45-46

Questions for Reflection
- How would you describe the image of Jesus you see in this week's readings from John?

- Imagine yourself at the tomb of Lazarus when you hear Jesus say in John 11:44, "Unbind him, and let him go." What would have been your reaction?

Viewing the Video: Session 6, Part 1
Follow this procedure for using this video: **Silence:** Clear your mind in anticipation of receiving a new insight from a fresh hearing of God's Word. **Listening:** Pay attention to the images and listen carefully to the narrative. **Discussion:** Use the following set of questions for guiding the group's responses.

John 11:17-44
- What feelings did the images evoke for you?

- How did the art you viewed "interpret" the Scripture you heard?

- What new insight(s) into the passage did the video provide?

Encountering God's Word in the Text

(20–25 minutes)

John 12:20-50 is a text that signals the beginning of the end for Jesus. Interestingly, upon hearing that the "Greeks" have come and wish to see him, Jesus declares, "The hour has come." In groups of three or four, explore this passage to locate: (1) messages that point to Jesus' death: (2) messages of judgment; and (3) messages of hope. After they spend time identifying the three kinds of messages, have the group discuss these questions:

- What common theme connects the three types of messages?

- Taken together, what do these messages say about Jesus?

- What do you think "They did not believe in him" (12:37) means?

- What is your understanding of John 12:39-40?

- How does Jesus' use of the image of the grain of wheat dying inform your understanding of Christ's death? Your understanding of your own death?

Form two new groups to examine the two very different situations where Jesus appears in John 12:1-19. One situation is very intimate, the other very public. Assign one group the story of the anointing in John 12:1-11. Assign the other group the story of Jesus' triumphal arrival in John 12:12-19. Instruct both groups to pay attention to and discuss the details of the stories using these questions.

- Who is present?

- What history do the main characters have with Jesus, and how does that history of relationship affect the story?

- What do the stories convey from a sensory perspective: smell, taste, touch, sound, and sight?

- How is Jesus portrayed in the story?

❖ In this week's readings, what did you "see" in Jesus? How did Jesus reveal God's glory? How do you understand Jesus as "the Word made flesh"?

Examining God's Word in Context

(15–20 minutes)

Christ does the miracle, but then he invites humans to assist him in bringing new life.

Viewing the Video: Session 6, Part 2

The focus in this section is on viewing Part 2 of the video. This video features two conversations: The first one involves biblical scholar Jaime Clark-Soles, and the second one takes place among a small group. Both conversations center around some portion of the week's readings in John and address a particular topic that emerges from them. One feature of each of the Part 2 video segments is an emphasis on a key "question" in the text and an "invitation" or declaration that Jesus provides in response to that question. **Both conversations run back-to-back and are meant to be viewed without pausing between them.**

Prepare to View Video

Note the context of the question directed toward Jesus in John 11:37, "Could not he who opened the eyes of the blind man have kept this man from dying?" and Jesus' response in John 11:40, "Did I not tell you that if you believed, you would see the glory of God?" Have group members locate the two verses in their Bibles before starting the video. Also listen for what is said about ideas related to faith, death, and life.

Discuss After Viewing Video

Follow up the two conversations in the video with questions such as "What insight from the scholar(s) or the small group caught your attention and why?" or "How did the conversation(s) inform your understanding of the week's reading?" In addition, consider using the following questions for further discussion.

• How does the raising of Lazarus prepare the reader for the resurrection of Jesus? How does the anointing of Jesus' feet prepare the reader for the washing of the disciples' feet?

- Jesus' words of invitation "I am the resurrection and the life" seem to speak about more than simply a physical death. How do these words bring us hope here and now and enable us to see the glory of God?

- How can we as believers in Christ help free others to receive this promise of new life?

- How does the saying "God may not come when you want him, but he's always right on time" express what the raising of Lazarus story teaches?

- When have we come to Jesus with a question like Mary and Martha had: "If only you'd been here, this wouldn't have happened"?

Going Forth With God's Word: An Invitation to Discipleship

(10–15 minutes)

Often our discipleship develops out of a careful process of assessing whether or not we can believe our eyes. Discipleship always involves an element of trust. In pairs, discuss the following questions:

- Along your spiritual journey, what have you discovered is necessary for you to be convinced about a new idea or interpretation?

- Share a moment when you have seen God's glory revealed.

- Share your thoughts on death and eternal life and how they have changed over time.

Call attention to the "For Reflection" section on page 82 in the participant book. Ask pairs to share responses to the questions.

If time permits, conclude this section of the group meeting by inviting persons to share their thoughts about the information printed in the participant book on page 83 under "For Further Reflection."

Closing and Prayer

Turn to Session 7, and review the focus of the lesson and the assignments for the week ahead. Establish a pattern of inviting prayer concerns and praying.

Would You Believe It?

Gathering Around God's Word

(15–20 minutes)

Welcome
Begin on time by welcoming the group to the study.

Prayer
Pray together as you begin your study.

Invitation From Scripture
So if I, your Lord and Teacher, have washed your feet, you also ought to wash one another's feet. —John 13:14

Questions for Reflection
- How would you describe the image of Jesus you see in this week's readings from John?

- Where were you the last time you participated in a foot-washing ceremony or heard spoken Jesus' words "Do not let your hearts be troubled" (14:1)?

Viewing the Video: Session 7, Part 1
Follow this procedure for using this video: **Silence:** Clear your mind in anticipation of receiving a new insight from a fresh hearing of God's Word. **Listening:** Pay attention to the images and listen carefully to the narrative. **Discussion:** Use the following set of questions for guiding the group's responses.

John 13:1-17; 14:1-12
- What feelings did the images evoke for you?

- How did the art you viewed "interpret" the Scripture you heard?

- What new insight(s) into the passage did the video provide?

Encountering God's Word in the Text

(20–25 minutes)

The disciples' love for each other is modeled after the love Jesus has demonstrated (and will demonstrate) for them. This mutual love is the sign of our discipleship for others to see.

Form two groups to explore two particular conversations Jesus has with his disciples. Assign one group John 13:31-38 and a second group John 14:15-24. Have each group study its assigned Scripture and paraphrase it in as few words as possible. Then, based on that paraphrase, ask each group to come up with a way to complete the following statement: "Love is...." Allow time to hear each group's paraphrase and completed statement in the total group.

Having examined how Jesus *talks* about love, spend time considering how Jesus *acts* in love in John's Gospel. Instruct the two groups to recall from the first thirteen chapters of the Gospel some of the events that highlight Jesus' love in action. For each event, discuss the following:

- Why did Jesus perform this act of love?

- How did the people around Jesus respond to this act of love?

- What did Jesus expect his disciples to learn from this act of love?

Consider comparing John's version of Jesus' last supper (13:1-30) with the account in the Synoptic Gospels. In the total group, share and discuss the notes and responses individuals made to the instructions listed in the Day 2 daily assignment section of the participant book on page 86.

❖ **In this week's readings, what did you "see" in Jesus? How did Jesus reveal God's glory? How do you understand Jesus as "the Word made flesh"?**

Examining God's Word in Context

(15–20 minutes)

The power of what follows the meal in John 13 results from the fact that Jesus has just washed Judas's feet, and now Judas leaves to arrange his master's arrest. Jesus has also washed Peter's feet, and soon Peter will deny him three times. Two so close to Jesus appear to be so far from him!

Viewing the Video: Session 7, Part 2

The focus in this section is on viewing Part 2 of the video. This video features two conversations: The first one takes place among biblical scholars Susan Hylen and Craig Koester, and the second one involves a small group. Both conversations center around some portion of the week's readings in John and address a particular topic that emerges from them. One feature of each of the Part 2 video segments is an emphasis on a key "question" in the text and an "invitation" or declaration that Jesus provides in response to that question. **Both conversations run back-to-back and are meant to be viewed without pausing between them.**

Prepare to View Video

Note the context of the question directed toward Jesus in John 13:6, "Lord, are you going to wash my feet?" and Jesus' response in John 13:8, "Unless I wash you, you have no share with me." Also note the context of the question directed toward Jesus in John 14:5, "Lord, we do not know where you are going. How can we know the way?" and Jesus' response in John 14:6, "I am the way." Have group members locate the verses in their Bibles before starting the video.

Discuss After Viewing Video

Follow up the two conversations in the video with questions such as "What insight from the scholar(s) or the small group caught your attention and why?" or "How did the conversation(s) inform your understanding of the week's reading?" In addition, consider using the following questions for further discussion.

- How does understanding Jesus washing the disciples' feet as a form of power define the nature of discipleship?

- If we view Jesus' declaration "I am the way, and the truth, and the life" as an answer, what is the question?

- Which do you find easier, washing someone's feet or having your own feet washed? Why? What are other ways we can "wash one another's feet"?

- When Jesus says, "Unless I wash you, you have no share with me," what does he mean?

Going Forth With God's Word:
An Invitation to Discipleship

(10–15 minutes)

Discipleship requires that sometimes we say, "I don't know," or "Would you believe it?" Like Jesus' first disciples, we are often just as prone to misunderstanding, superficiality, and failure as they were. In pairs, discuss the following questions:

• What does the idea that Jesus is "the way of cross and resurrection" mean to you?

• What are the most persistent questions you continue to encounter in your faith journey?

• When in your life have you said to someone, "Would you believe it if I told you...?" How did you complete the question? How did the individual hearing your question respond?

• Where in your discipleship do you still feel inadequate, uncertain, or prone to failure?

Call attention to the "For Reflection" section on page 94 in the participant book. Ask pairs to share responses to the questions.

If time permits, conclude this section of the group meeting by inviting persons to share their thoughts about the information printed in the participant book on page 95 under "For Further Reflection."

Closing and Prayer

Turn to Session 8, and review the focus of the lesson and the assignments for the week ahead. Establish a pattern of inviting prayer concerns and praying together at this time.

What Time Is It? SESSION

8

Gathering Around God's Word

(15–20 minutes)

Welcome
Begin on time by welcoming the group to the study.

Prayer
Pray together as you begin your study.

Invitation From Scripture
I have said these things to you in figures of speech. The hour is coming when I will no longer speak to you in figures, but will tell you plainly of the Father.
—John 16:25

Questions for Reflection
- How would you describe the image of Jesus you see in this week's readings from John?

- When have you been fearful of being abandoned or had to leave behind some place or some person?

Viewing the Video: Session 8, Part 1
Follow this procedure for using this video: **Silence:** Clear your mind in anticipation of receiving a new insight from a fresh hearing of God's Word. **Listening:** Pay attention to the images and listen carefully to the narrative. **Discussion:** Use the following set of questions for guiding the group's responses.

John 16:7-33
- What feelings did the images evoke for you?

- How did the art you viewed "interpret" the Scripture you heard?

- What new insight(s) into the passage did the video provide?

Encountering God's Word in the Text

(20–25 minutes)

In John 15, the vine is an allegory to suggest the complex relationship among Jesus, God, and the believer. God is the vinegrower, Jesus is the vine, and believers are the branches. As inviting an image as it was, the disciples struggled to understand the implications of it. In fact, they had trouble comprehending all that Jesus wanted to tell them, especially when he talked about leaving them.

Examine this portion of the "Farewell Discourses" by first listening to John 15:1-17 read aloud. Then, in groups of three or four, discuss the following questions:

- How is the life of Jesus' disciples similar to the relationship between a vine and its branches?

- What does the word *abide* bring to mind? According to Jesus, what are the benefits of "abiding"?

- What does the word *prune* bring to mind? In the Christian life, how does "pruning" occur, and what are often the results?

- What is the correlation between loving others and abiding in the vine?

Now turn the two groups' attention to John 15:18–16:4a. Call attention to the shift from love in the previous verses to hate in these verses.

- What are the words of warning, and why are they given? Based on the criteria in 15:19, what is it about a follower of Christ that the world hates?

- How well do you think we as Christians today live up to this criteria?

- What words of assurance are given in this passage?

If time allows, talk about the group's understanding of the Paraclete in John.

- To what extent do we experience the Holy Spirit as an Advocate, as someone who comes alongside us?

❖ **In this week's readings, what did you "see" in Jesus? How did Jesus reveal God's glory? How do you understand Jesus as "the Word made flesh"?**

Examining God's Word in Context

(15–20 minutes)

By our side in this struggle in the world, the Paraclete whispers in our ears the truth of God's presence in Christ. The Spirit's work fills the gap left by Jesus' going away.

Viewing the Video: Session 8, Part 2

The focus in this section is on viewing Part 2 of the video. This video features two conversations: The first one involves biblical scholar Ben Witherington, and the second one takes place among a small group. Both conversations center around some portion of the week's readings in John and address a particular topic that emerges from them. One feature of each of the Part 2 video segments is an emphasis on a key "question" in the text and an "invitation" or declaration that Jesus provides in response to that question. **Both conversations run back-to-back and are meant to be viewed without pausing between them.**

Prepare to View Video

Note the context of the question directed toward Jesus in John 16:18, "What does he mean by this 'a little while'?" and Jesus' response in John 16:22, "I will see you again, and your hearts will rejoice." Have group members locate the two verses in their Bibles before starting the video. Also listen for what is said regarding Jesus' promise of the Holy Spirit and the difficulty the disciples had in comprehending that promise.

Discuss After Viewing Video

Follow up the two conversations in the video with questions such as "What insight from the scholar(s) or the small group caught your attention and why?" or "How did the conversation(s) inform your understanding of the week's reading?" In addition, consider using the following questions for further discussion.

- To what extent do you think the woman in labor analogy helped the disciples understand Jesus' point?

- When are we guilty of looking to Jesus to meet our expectations rather than our needs?

- What are the disciples asking when they say, "What does he mean by this 'a little while'?" What are their real concerns, and how are they our concerns as well?

- When have you viewed an experience of pain or struggle as a sign of God's abandonment or as an indication of having fallen out of God's favor? Where or how did you eventually find comfort or assurance?

Going Forth With God's Word: An Invitation to Discipleship

(10–15 minutes)

Life in this world corners us and demands our decision. Discipleship means choosing God's love and acceptance as our highest priority every minute of every day.

Have everyone turn to the "For Reflection" section on page 105 in the participant book, and invite persons to share the summary they wrote in response to the instructions.

Then, in pairs, discuss the following questions:

- How would you describe the role the Holy Spirit plays in your life?

- How do you manage your time on a regular basis, both the *chronos* kind and the *kairos* kind? (See page 52 in the participant book for the marginal note that defines the two terms.) What do you think would happen if you invited the Paraclete, the Holy Spirit, to come alongside you and guide your use of time?

If time permits, conclude this section of the group meeting by inviting persons to share their thoughts about the information printed in the participant book on page 106 under "For Further Reflection."

Closing and Prayer

Turn to Session 9, and review the focus of the lesson and the assignments for the week ahead. Establish a pattern of inviting prayer concerns and praying together at this time.

Look Out!

Gathering Around God's Word

(15–20 minutes)

Welcome
Begin on time by welcoming the group to the study.

Prayer
Pray together as you begin your study.

Invitation From Scripture
They came there with lanterns and torches and weapons. Then Jesus, knowing all that was to happen to him, came forward and asked them, "Whom are you looking for?" They answered, "Jesus of Nazareth." Jesus replied, "I am he." ...They stepped back and fell to the ground.   —John 18:3-6

Questions for Reflection
- How would you describe the image of Jesus you see in this week's readings from John?

- Note the similarity between Jesus' query in John 18:4, "Whom are you looking for?" and his earlier question in John 1:38, "What are you looking for?" What is the connection John wants you to make?

Viewing the Video: Session 9, Part 1
Follow this procedure for using this video: **Silence:** Clear your mind in anticipation of receiving a new insight from a fresh hearing of God's Word. **Listening:** Pay attention to the images and listen carefully to the narrative. **Discussion:** Use the following set of questions for guiding the group's responses.

John 18:28–19:16a
- What feelings did the images evoke for you?

- How did the art you viewed "interpret" the Scripture you heard?

- What new insight(s) into the passage did the video provide?

Encountering God's Word in the Text

(20–25 minutes)

If *glorification* is the revelation of God's presence in the world, Jesus is asking that God manifest God's self through his suffering and death. It is a mutual glorification, because if God's presence shines through Jesus, then both are glorified.

In groups of three or four, explore Jesus' prayer in John 17.

- Consider the chapter in three sections: 17:1-5; 17:6-19; and 17:20-26. What is the subject of Jesus' prayer in each section? What themes underlie the whole prayer in John 17?

- What is your understanding of glorification? What does the abundant use of "glorify" in Jesus' language mean to you?

Compare and contrast Jesus' prayer in 17:20-26 with Jesus' prayer in the garden of Gethsemane as recorded in the other Gospels (Matthew 26:36-46; Mark 14:32-42; Luke 22:40-46).

Listen to John 18:1-14 (Jesus' arrest) read aloud. In the total group, discuss the differences between this account in John and the parallel accounts in the other Gospels (Matthew 26:47-56; Mark 14:43-51; Luke 22:47-54).

- What themes appear in John that do not appear in the Synoptic accounts?

- What aspects of the story stand out the most?

Form two groups to examine the story of Peter's denial of Jesus in John 18:15-27. Use these questions to guide discussion:

- What is the significance of the contrast between Peter's denial and Jesus' faithfulness?

- How does this story support the message of the Gospel of John?

- What do you think happened between Peter's boldness in John 18:10-11 and his weakness in this passage?

❖ **In this week's readings, what did you "see" in Jesus? How did Jesus reveal God's glory? How do you understand Jesus as "the Word made flesh"?**

Examining God's Word in Context

(15–20 minutes)

Sanctified, the disciples have been sent into the world in the same way God sent Christ into the world.

Viewing the Video: Session 9, Part 2

The focus in this section is on viewing Part 2 of the video. This video features two conversations: The first one involves biblical scholar Jaime Clark-Soles, and the second one takes place among a small group. Both conversations center around some portion of the week's readings in John and address a particular topic that emerges from them. One feature of each of the Part 2 video segments is an emphasis on a key "question" in the text and an "invitation" or declaration that Jesus provides in response to that question. **Both conversations run back-to-back and are meant to be viewed without pausing between them.**

Prepare to View Video

Note the context of the question directed toward Jesus in John 18:33, "Are you the King of the Jews?" and Jesus' response in John 18:36, "My kingdom is not from this world." Have group members locate the two verses in their Bibles before starting the video.

Discuss After Viewing Video

Follow up the two conversations in the video with questions such as "What insight from the scholar(s) or the small group caught your attention and why?" or "How did the conversation(s) inform your understanding of the week's reading?" In addition, consider using the following questions for further discussion.

• What is behind Pilate's question "Are you the King of the Jews?" Do you think we should take Pilate's question "What is truth?" as searching or as sarcastic? Why?

• How do you think John's Jesus would have answered the question regarding truth? What does it mean that Jesus did not answer that question in particular? How would you have answered that question for Jesus?

- What is the kingdom Jesus refers to as "the kingdom that is not from this world"?

- What are some of the characteristics of that kingdom as exemplified in the life of Christ?

- In what way is kingdom living radical obedience?

Going Forth With God's Word: An Invitation to Discipleship

(10–15 minutes)

Discipleship can lead us to death—the death of our luxury, our independence, our reputation, or our tranquility.

In pairs, discuss the following questions:

- In what ways are you bringing glory to the name of Christ and doing the work you have been called to do?

- What would you say you have given up in the name of discipleship?

Call attention to the "For Reflection" section on page 116 in the participant book. Ask pairs to share responses to the questions.

If time permits, conclude this section of the group meeting by inviting persons to share their thoughts about the information printed in the participant book on page 117 under "For Further Reflection."

Closing and Prayer

Turn to Session 10, and review the focus of the lesson and the assignments for the week ahead. Establish a pattern of inviting prayer concerns and praying together at this time.

Believing Without Seeing

Gathering Around God's Word

(15–20 minutes)

Welcome
Begin on time by welcoming the group to the study.

Prayer
Pray together as you begin your study.

Invitation From Scripture
Jesus said to him [Thomas], "Have you believed because you have seen me? Blessed are those who have not seen and yet have come to believe." —John 20:29

Questions for Reflection
- How would you describe the image of Jesus you see in this week's readings from John?

- What doubts have you had or confronted related to Christ's resurrection?

Viewing the Video: Session 10, Part 1
Follow this procedure for using this video: **Silence:** Clear your mind in anticipation of receiving a new insight from a fresh hearing of God's Word. **Listening:** Pay attention to the images and listen carefully to the narrative. **Discussion:** Use the following set of questions for guiding the group's responses.

John 20:1-21
- What feelings did the images evoke for you?

- How did the art you viewed "interpret" the Scripture you heard?

- What new insight(s) into the passage did the video provide?

Encountering God's Word in the Text

(20–25 minutes)

For John, Jesus is the new Passover Lamb who brings a new exodus from sin and death. John's understanding of the cross is rooted in the meaning of the Passover.

Form two or three groups to examine John 19:1-16. Use these questions for discussion:

- What are the motives of Pilate?

- What kind of emotions does Pilate show?

- What causes a change in his motives and/or emotions?

- What do you make of the way Jesus responds to Pilate?

- What does Jesus mean by saying, "The one who handed me over to you is guilty of a greater sin" (19:11)?

- What does John want us to see in the crowd's response to Jesus' trial?

Call attention to the Day 2 instructions in the daily assignment section on page 120 in the participant book. In the same two or three groups, listen to responses comparing John 19:17-42 with the accounts of Jesus' crucifixion in the Synoptic Gospels (Matthew 27:33-66; Mark 15:22-47; Luke 23:33-56). Then come together in the total group and talk about (1) the uniqueness of John's way of narrating the story of the Crucifixion and (2) how he uses the meaning of the Passover to assign significance to the story.

One way to approach John 19–20 is to focus on the principle characters and their relationship to Jesus. While John shares much in common with the other Gospels, he is unique in the focus he gives to Jesus' encounters with Pilate, Mary Magdalene, and Thomas in these two chapters. Invite people to imagine themselves as one of those three characters and declare who Jesus is from that character's perspective.

❖ **In this week's readings, what did you "see" in Jesus? How did Jesus reveal God's glory? How do you understand Jesus as "the Word made flesh"?**

51

Examining God's Word in Context

(15–20 minutes)

We cannot hold on to Jesus and keep him to ourselves. The risen Christ has another mission.

Viewing the Video: Session 10, Part 2

The focus in this section is on viewing Part 2 of the video. This video features two conversations: The first one involves biblical scholar Ben Witherington, and the second one takes place among a small group. Both conversations center around some portion of the week's readings in John and address a particular topic that emerges from them. One feature of each of the Part 2 video segments is an emphasis on a key "question" in the text and an "invitation" or declaration that Jesus provides in response to that question. **Both conversations run back-to-back and are meant to be viewed without pausing between them.**

Prepare to View Video

Note the context of the question directed toward Mary in John 20:13, "Woman, why are you weeping?" and Jesus' four responses in John 20:16-19, "Mary...do not hold on to me.... But go.... Peace be with you." Have group members locate the verses in their Bibles before starting the video. Listen also for what is said about seeing and believing.

Discuss After Viewing Video

Follow up the two conversations in the video with questions such as "What insight from the scholar(s) or the small group caught your attention and why?" or "How did the conversation(s) inform your understanding of the week's reading?" In addition, consider using the following questions for further discussion.

- In John 20, what do the actions and words of Mary Magdalene, the "other disciple," and Peter on Easter morning reveal about their understanding of Jesus and their relationship with him?

- What is the significance of the angels' question, "Woman, why are you weeping?"

- How does Jesus' response "Do not hold on to me" relate to your understanding of the angels' question? How does John want us as readers to hear that imperative? What's wrong with clinging to Jesus?

- When Jesus meets with the disciples, he offers them peace. What is significant about Christ's gift of peace for them at that time? What is the significance of that gift for the church today? For each of us?

Going Forth With God's Word: An Invitation to Discipleship

(10–15 minutes)

We cannot help but wish that we could "come and see" Jesus as the first disciples did. However, we are left with the task of learning to believe without seeing.

Form pairs and read aloud John 20:11-17. Then discuss the following questions:

- When has Jesus, in a way, called you by name?

- What was your response to that calling?

In the same pairs, read aloud John 20:24-31. Then discuss the following questions:

- Thomas's statement of faith was "My Lord and my God!" (20:28). What is your statement of faith in Jesus?

- What makes it most difficult in your own life of faith to believe without seeing?

Call attention to the "For Reflection" section on page 128 in the participant book. Ask pairs to share responses to the questions.

If time permits, conclude this section of the group meeting by inviting persons to share their thoughts about the information printed in the participant book on page 129 under "For Further Reflection."

Closing and Prayer

Turn to Session 11, and review the focus of the lesson and the assignments for the week ahead. Establish a pattern of inviting prayer concerns and praying together at this time.

Do You See Him?

Gathering Around God's Word

(15–20 minutes)

Welcome
Begin on time by welcoming the group to the study.

Prayer
Pray together as you begin your study.

Invitation From Scripture
Just after daybreak, Jesus stood on the beach; but the disciples did not know that it was Jesus.... That disciple whom Jesus loved said to Peter, "It is the Lord!"
—John 21:4, 7

Questions for Reflection
- How would you describe the image of Jesus you see in this week's readings from John?

- When have you found yourself surprised by a sudden awareness of Christ presence?

Viewing the Video: Session 11, Part 1
Follow this procedure for using this video: **Silence:** Clear your mind in anticipation of receiving a new insight from a fresh hearing of God's Word. **Listening:** Pay attention to the images and listen carefully to the narrative. **Discussion:** Use the following set of questions for guiding the group's responses.

John 21:1-19
- What feelings did the images evoke for you?

- How did the art you viewed "interpret" the Scripture you heard?

- What new insight(s) into the passage did the video provide?

Encountering God's Word in the Text

(20–25 minutes)

John seems determined to drive home the point to his readers that Christ's nearness coincides with their neediness. In groups of three or four, discuss the following questions:

- Why do you think some of the disciples decided to go fishing?

- Jesus calls out, "Children, you have no fish, have you?" (21:5). What more might Jesus have meant with that question?

- Recalling that Jesus said to his disciples, "My sheep hear my voice. I know them, and they follow me" (10:27), why do you think the disciples don't recognize Jesus when he calls out to them?

- Why is it that Jesus is recognized only when the nets are full? What does Peter's response communicate? What significance do you see in the number of fish caught?

The first conversation we hear between Peter and Jesus is in John 21:15-19. This conversation follows Peter jumping out of the boat to meet Jesus and everyone gathering around the fire to eat breakfast.

- Based on Peter's previous actions, imagine what he might have said to Jesus before this final dialogue. Imagine how he must have felt: Ashamed? Relieved? Apprehensive? Incredulous?

- What is John trying to tell us by including this dialogue? What does John 21:20-25 add to the conversation?

❖ **In this week's readings, what did you "see" in Jesus? How did Jesus reveal God's glory? How do you understand Jesus as "the Word made flesh"?**

Examining God's Word in Context

(15–20 minutes)

As followers of Christ, we are one with one another at levels far deeper than acquaintance or friendship. Our devotion to Christ and God is singular, and our mission to the world is singular.

Viewing the Video: Session 11, Part 2

The focus in this section is on viewing Part 2 of the video. This video features two conversations: The first one involves biblical scholar Craig Koester, and the second one takes place among a small group. Both conversations center around some portion of the week's readings in John and address a particular topic that emerges from them. One feature of each of the Part 2 video segments is an emphasis on a key "question" in the text and an "invitation" or declaration that Jesus provides in response to that question. **Both conversations run back-to-back and are meant to be viewed without pausing between them.**

Prepare to View Video

Note the context of the question directed toward Peter in John 21:17, "Do you love me?" and Peter's response in the same verse, "Lord, you know everything; you know that I love you." Also note Jesus' response, "Feed my sheep." Have group members locate the verse in their Bibles before starting the video. Listen for what is said about the implications of Jesus' response for believers today.

Discuss After Viewing Video

Follow up the two conversations in the video with questions such as "What insight from the scholar(s) or the small group caught your attention and why?" or "How did the conversation(s) inform your understanding of the week's reading?" In addition, consider using the following questions for further discussion.

- Why do you think it is important in John's Gospel that Jesus meet the disciples in the ordinary? How does Jesus meet us in the ordinary?

- What do you hear beneath the response given by Peter, "Lord, you know everything; you know that I love you"? What often lies beneath our responses to Jesus' question "Do you love me?"

- Jesus calls Peter to the unglamorous tasks of being a shepherd to others. What are the unglamorous tasks to which Jesus calls us?

- The disciples began following Jesus when he said to them, "Come and see" (1:39). Between these words and Jesus' final invitation, "Follow me!" (21:22), recall some of the works and wonders the disciples have seen Jesus do.

- Recall you own journey between Christ's initial invitation and where you are now. What works of Jesus have you seen?

- What is the hardest aspect of choosing to love the way Jesus wants us to love?

Going Forth With God's Word: An Invitation to Discipleship

(10–15 minutes)

Christian discipleship entails a conviction that Christ remains active in our world today through the agency of those who believe in him. Following Jesus means more than simply acknowledging that Christ fulfills the basic needs of humans. It means becoming actively engaged in seeking to fulfill those needs today—that is, we become the hands, the words, and the deeds of Christ today.

In pairs, discuss the following questions:

- If Christ were to ask you, "Do you love me more than these?" what would he be referring to? Your job, your family, your hobbies, your habits? What else?

- In your study of John, how has Jesus become "the Word made flesh" to you? What "word" describes Jesus to you?

- Of the eight principles listed under the "Invitation to Discipleship" section in the participant book (pages 137–39), which do you resonate with and why? What features of the discipleship called for in John would you add to this list?

- How would you describe your mission or calling as you obey Jesus' invitation "Follow me"?

Call attention to the "For Reflection" section on page 140 in the participant book. Ask pairs to share responses to the last two questions.

If time permits, conclude this section of the group meeting by inviting persons to share their thoughts about the information printed in the participant book on page 141 under "For Further Reflection."

Closing and Prayer

Thank the participants for their participation. Make any announcements that are needed. Consider singing or reciting the words to a hymn as part of the closing. Some recommended hymns are:

- "Lord, You Have Come to the Lakeshore"
- "I Have Decided to Follow Jesus"
- "I Come With Joy"
- "Savior, Like a Shepherd Lead Us"

Then close with prayer.

Special note: As part of your closing, plan to schedule a time with your group to view the 2003 film *The Gospel of John*, a recent installment in The Visual Bible series. The film is available in DVD format and comes in two versions, one running two hours and the full theatrical version running about three hours (see http://www.visualbible.com for more information). Because the film's screenplay is the complete Today's English Version (TEV) of the Bible (the Good News Bible), group members familiar with the text and narrative sequence of the Gospel should find viewing the film a meaningful complement to their study together.

Video Art Credits

Opening Sequence

Jesus and the Samaritan Woman, by Dr. He Qi (www.heqigallery.com).

Feeding of the 5000, by Laura James, © Private Collection / The Bridgeman Art Library International.

The Resurrection of Lazarus, by Henry Ossawa Tanner, Erich Lessing / Art Resource, NY.

Ecce Homo, by Antonio Ciseri © Galleria d'Arte Moderna, Florence, Italy / The Bridgeman Art Library International.

Christ appears to Saint Mary Magdalen, by Laurent de La Hyre, Erich Lessing / Art Resource, NY.

The Great Catch, by John August Swanson. Used by permission of the artist (www.johnaugustswanson.com).

Holy Ghost, by Giusto de Menabuoi, Alinari / Art Resource, NY.

Session 1—John 1:35-51

Christ on the Mountain, by Arnold C. Slade © SuperStock, Inc. / SuperStock.

The Calling of Andrew and John, by James Tissot © SuperStock, Inc. / SuperStock.

Jesus Goes Up to Jerusalem, by James Tissot © SuperStock, Inc. / SuperStock.

Calling of the Disciples, by Dr. He Qi (www.heqigallery.com).

The Calling of Peter & Andrew, by James Tissot © SuperStock, Inc. / SuperStock.

The Calling of Saints Peter and Andrew, early Christian mosaic (6th CE), Scala / Art Resource, NY.

Christ Calling his Disciples, by Adam Brenner © New Walk Museum, Leicester City Museum Service, UK / The Bridgeman Art Library.

Session 2—John 4:1-30

Jesus on His Way to Galilee, by James Tissot © SuperStock, Inc. / SuperStock.

The Woman of Samaria, by William Dyce © Birmingham Museums and Art Gallery / The Bridgeman Art Library.

The Woman of Samaria, by Carl Heinrich Bloch © SuperStock, Inc. / SuperStock.

Christ and the Samaritan Woman at the Well, by Jacopo Robusti Tintoretto, Scala / Art Resource, NY.

The Samaritan Woman at the Well, by Jacopo Robusti Tintoretto, Scala / Art Resource, NY.

Jesus and the Samaritan Woman, by Dr. He Qi (www.heqigallery.com).

The Samaritan woman at the well, early Christian mosaic, Erich Lessing / Art Resource, NY.

The Samaritan Woman, by Georges Rouault © Peter Willi / SuperStock.

The Samaritan Woman at the Well, by Dr. He Qi (www.heqigallery.com).

The Woman of Samaria, by Yu Jiade © Asian Christian Art Association.

Session 3—John 6:1-14, 25-40

Seek Me Because Ye Eat from the Loaves, by James Tissot © SuperStock, Inc. / SuperStock.

Miracle of the Loaves and Fishes, by James Tissot © SuperStock, Inc. / SuperStock.

Jesus and the multiplication of bread and fish, four apostles, 6th Century mosaic, Erich Lessing / Art Resource, NY.

Jesus and the multiplication of the bread, an apostle, and a man with bread baskets, 6th Century mosaic, Erich Lessing / Art Resource, NY.

Feeding of the 5000, by Laura James © Private Collection / The Bridgeman Art Library International.

Christ and the multiplication of the loaves and the fish, by Gaspard de Crayer, Réunion des Musées Nationaux / Art Resource, NY.

The Multiplication of the Loaves and Fishes, by Giovanni Lanfranco © National Gallery of Ireland, Dublin, Ireland / The Bridgeman Art Library.

Session 4—John 8:13a, 19-20, 31-47, 52-59

Pharisees, by Karl Schmidt-Rottluff © SuperStock, Inc. / SuperStock.

Pharisees Question Jesus, by James Tissot © SuperStock, Inc. / SuperStock.

Jesus Speaking to the Treasury, by James Tissot © SuperStock, Inc. / SuperStock.

Detail of a group watching Christ healing the possessed, Late-Ottonian fresco cycle, before 1090, Erich Lessing / Art Resource, NY.

The Pharisees And Sadducees Come To Tempt Jesus, by James Tissot © SuperStock, Inc. / SuperStock.

Christ Reproving the Pharisees, by James Tissot © SuperStock, Inc. / SuperStock.

The Pharisees Conspire Together, by James Tissot © SuperStock, Inc. / SuperStock.

Pharisees & Herodians Take Counsel Against Jesus, by James Tissot © SuperStock, Inc. / SuperStock.

Jesus in the Temple, by Giovanni Paolo Panini © SuperStock, Inc. / SuperStock.

But No Man Laid Hands Upon Him, by James Tissot © SuperStock, Inc. / SuperStock.

Session 5—John 9:1-41

Christ healing the blind at Jericho, by Nicolas Poussin, Réunion des Musées Nationaux / Art Resource, NY.

The Man Born Blind, by Carl Heinrich Bloch © SuperStock, Inc. / SuperStock.

In the Villages, the Sick were Brought out to Him, by James Tissot © SuperStock, Inc. / SuperStock.

The man born blind, by Jesus Mafa © Jesus Mafa.

Blind Man Washes in the Pool of Siloam, by James Tissot © SuperStock, Inc. / SuperStock.

The Miracle of Christ Healing the Blind, by El Greco © SuperStock, Inc. / SuperStock.

Christ healing the blind men of Jericho, early Christian mosaic (6th CE), Scala / Art Resource, NY.

Miracle of the Blind Born (Christ healing the blind), by Domenico Passignano, Scala / Art Resource, NY.

Hand of Jesus touching a blind man's eye; detail of "Two blind men cured", Early Christian mosaic (6th CE). Scala / Art Resource, NY.

The Healing of the Blind Man, by El Greco, Scala / Art Resource, NY.

He That Has Seen Me, Has Seen the Father, by James Tissot © SuperStock, Inc. / SuperStock.

Session 6—John 11:17-44

The Raising of Lazarus, by Sebastiano del Piombo © SuperStock, Inc. / SuperStock.

Christ in Martha's House, by Diego Velázquez © SuperStock, Inc. / SuperStock.

Christ in the House of Martha and Mary, by Jan Vermeer © SuperStock, Inc. / SuperStock.

The Resurrection of Lazarus, by Leon Bonnat, Réunion des Musées Nationaux / Art Resource, NY.

Martha and Mary telling Jesus of the death of Lazarus, Ms Lat. Q.v.I.126 f.69v, from the 'Book of Hours of Louis d'Orleans', by Jean Colombe © National Library, St. Petersburg, Russia / The Bridgeman Art Library.

Resurrection of Lazarus, by Jean Baptiste Corneille, Giraudon / Art Resource, NY.

The Resurrection of Lazarus, by Henry Ossawa Tanner, Erich Lessing / Art Resource, NY.

Session 7—John 13:1-17; 14:1-12

Disciples Admire the Buildings of the Temple, by James Tissot © SuperStock, Inc. / SuperStock.

Jesus Washing the Feet of his Disciples, by Albert Gustaf Aristides Edelfelt © Nationalmuseum, Stockholm, Sweden / The Bridgeman Art Library.

Jesus Washing Peter's Feet, by Ford Madox Brown © SuperStock, Inc. / SuperStock.

Christ washing the feet of the Apostles, manuscript page (France, 12th–13th century), The Pierpont Morgan Library / Art Resource, NY.

Christ Washing the Disciples' Feet, by Adrian Kupman © SuperStock, Inc. / SuperStock.

Christ Washing the Disciples' Feet, School of Arezzo © Christie's Images / SuperStock.

The Washing of the Feet, by John August Swanson. Used by permission of the artist (www.johnaugustswanson.com).

Washing the Feet, by Jyoti Sahi © Asian Christian Art Association.

Jesus Washing the Disciples' Feet, by James Jacques Joseph Tissot © Brooklyn Museum of Art, New York, NY / The Bridgeman Art Library.

If All, Not I...., by Il'ja Efimovic Repin © Anatoly Sapronenkov / SuperStock.

Session 8—John 16:7-33

The Last Discourse Of Our Lord Jesus Christ, by James Tissot © SuperStock, Inc. / SuperStock.

Holy Ghost, by Giusto de Menabuoi, Alinari / Art Resource, NY.

Jesus and His Disciples, by Arturo Gordon Vargas © Kactus Foto / SuperStock.

Jesus Washing the Disciples' Feet, by James Jacques Joseph Tissot © Brooklyn Museum of Art, New York, NY / The Bridgeman Art Library.

Ascension of Our Lord, Pskov School (16th Century icons) © Leonid Bogdanov / SuperStock.

The Entombment by Theodore Gericault © Bridgeman Art Library, London / SuperStock.

Farewell of the Apostles. Panel from the back of the Maesta altarpiece, by Duccio, Scala / Art Resource, NY.

Mary Magdalene at the Sepulchre, by William Blake, Yale Center for British Art, Paul Mellon Collection, USA / The Bridgeman Art Library.

The Ascension, by Caserta Bazile © SuperStock, Inc. / SuperStock.

Session 9—John 18:28–19:16a

Christ Before Pilate, by Adrian Kupman © SuperStock, Inc. / SuperStock.

Ecce Homo, by Antonio Ciseri, Galleria d'Arte Moderna, Florence, Italy / The Bridgeman Art Library International.

What is the truth? (Christ before Pilate), by Nikolai Ge, Scala / Art Resource, NY.

Christ before Pilate, by Mihaly Munkacsy, Erich Lessing / Art Resource, NY.

Ecce Homo, by Mattia Preti, Réunion des Musées Nationaux / Art Resource, NY.

Jesus Insulted by the Soldier, by Jean Valentin de Boulogne © SuperStock, Inc. / SuperStock.

Pilate Announces Judgement from the Gabbatha, by James Tissot © SuperStock, Inc. / SuperStock.

Christ Presented to the People, by Quinten Metsys I © SuperStock, Inc. / SuperStock.

Session 10—John 20:1-21

Mary Magdalene in the Tomb, by James Tissot © SuperStock, Inc. / SuperStock.

He Appeared to the Eleven as They Sat at Meat, by James Tissot © SuperStock, Inc. / SuperStock.

Disciples Peter and John Rushing to the Sepulcher the Morning of the Resurrection, by Eugene Burnand © Peter Willi / SuperStock, Inc.

Mary Magdalene at the Sepulchre by William Blake, © Yale Center for British Art, Paul Mellon Collection, USA / The Bridgeman Art Library.

He is not here, He is risen, by Hanna Cheriyan Varghese. Used by permission of the artist (www.awrc4ct.org).

Christ appears to Saint Mary Magdalen, by Laurent de La Hyre, Erich Lessing / Art Resource, NY.

Noli me tangere, by Maurice Denis © ARS, NY / Erich Lessing / Art Resource, NY.

Noli me tangere. Saint Mary Magdalen encounters Christ after His resurrection, by Titian (Tiziano Vecellio), Erich Lessing / Art Resource, NY.

Christ Appearing to Mary, by Albert Pinkham Ryder, Smithsonian American Art Museum © SuperStock, Inc. / SuperStock.

Session 11—John 21:1-19

Christ Eating with his Disciples, by James Tissot © SuperStock, Inc. / SuperStock.

Peter Cast Himself into the Sea, by James Tissot © SuperStock, Inc. / SuperStock.

Feed My Lambs, by James Tissot © SuperStock, Inc. / SuperStock.

The Great Catch, by John August Swanson. Used by permission of the artist (www.johnaugustswanson.com).

Christ Appears on the Borders of the Tiberius Sea, by James Tissot © SuperStock, Inc. / SuperStock.

Crucifixion, by Kim Yong Gil © Asian Christian Art Association.

Literary Credit (Session 8, Part 2)

"That Holy Thing," by George MacDonald, in *Christ in Poetry: An Anthology*, compiled and edited by Thomas Curtis Clark and Hazel Davis Clark (Association Press: New York, 1952); page 20.